12/10

SOC.

THE U.S. INDUSTRIAL
REVOLUTION

Essential Events

The U.S. Industrial

Revolution

BY ROBERT GRAYSON

Content Consultant
J. D. Bowers, associate professor,
Department of History, Northern Illinois University

ABDO
Publishing Company

CREDITS

Published by ABDO Publishing Company, 8000 West 78th Street, Edina, Minnesota 55439. Copyright © 2011 by Abdo Consulting Group, Inc. International copyrights reserved in all countries. No part of this book may be reproduced in any form without written permission from the publisher. The Essential Library™ is a trademark and logo of ABDO Publishing Company.

Printed in the United States of America,
North Mankato, Minnesota
062010
092010

 THIS BOOK CONTAINS AT LEAST 10% RECYCLED MATERIALS.

Editor: Holly Saari
Copy Editor: Paula Lewis
Interior Design and Production: Christa Schneider
Cover Design: Kazuko Collins

Library of Congress Cataloging-in-Publication Data
Grayson, Robert, 1951-
  The U.S. industrial revolution / Robert Grayson.
    p. cm. — (Essential events)
  Includes bibliographical references and index.
  ISBN 978-1-61613-687-1
  1. Industrial revolution—United States—History—Juvenile literature. 2. Industries—United States—History—Juvenile literature. 3. United States—Economic conditions—Juvenile literature. I. Title.
  HC105.6.U7 2010
  330.973'05—dc22
                                            2010013516

The U.S. Industrial Revolution

TABLE OF CONTENTS

At the end of the eighteenth century, British law prevented people from taking textile-manufacturing secrets out of the country.

A Revolution Begins

In 1789, 21-year-old Samuel Slater was about to take a huge risk. The English businessman planned to take cloth-making secrets out of the country—an illegal act. Two years earlier, the British government had passed a law prohibiting anyone with knowledge of the textile industry and machinery to leave the nation. The government wanted to prevent other countries from learning the information that had made Great Britain so wealthy in recent years.

Slater told no one of his plans to leave England. If word spread, he would be jailed. He could not take papers documenting the details of his trade. Those would be found. Instead, he memorized all the information needed to build textile machinery and run the mills. His goal was to bring his knowledge to the recently formed United States. There, he hoped to start a textile business and become wealthy.

BEFORE THE INDUSTRIAL REVOLUTION

At the time of Slater's departure, life in England was undergoing a drastic change. Prior to the

Industrial Revolution Defined

An industrial revolution is when an economy changes from an agricultural, or farming, base to industry. Products go from being hand-crafted one by one to being mass-produced by machines. Many social changes are brought about by industrialization. The population shifts from rural to urban areas; the workforce becomes radically altered. The changes are so massive that historians believe the best way to describe their overall impact is to call the event a revolution.

eighteenth century, textile factories, or factories of any kind, did not exist. Farming was the biggest industry, and approximately 90 percent of people lived in rural areas. Most families made do on their own. They grew their food and made the other products they needed for daily life. Farming did not make them wealthy. Most families did not have enough to sell at the market—they had just enough for their own needs. The few craftspeople made products by hand in their homes or small shops, and they sold their goods only within their immediate village.

In the first few decades of the eighteenth century, the situation began to change. Three important changes combined to set the foundation for a revolution in industry: more effective farming practices, the rise of consumer goods, and scientific and technological advancements.

The Term *Industrial Revolution*

In 1884, British historian Albert Toynbee popularized the term *Industrial Revolution* to describe the period of change in Great Britain between 1760 and 1832. Toynbee described the change that happened in these years as dramatic and rapid—such as a revolution. Since then, however, the specific dates of the Industrial Revolution have come into question by historians.

Before the Industrial Revolution in Great Britain, most people lived in rural areas and worked on farms.

New farming methods allowed for more land to be used more often. Unusable swamplands could be drained and used for crops. New kinds of crops did away with the necessity of rotating crops every three years. The same farmland could be used each year, which increased food production.

The Potato

One of the crops that impacted the development of the Industrial Revolution was the potato. Potatoes originated in South America. Spanish explorers brought them back to Spain in the sixteenth century, and the crop spread across Europe. However, it was not popular. The taste was strange for many people.

Planting of potatoes increased in Great Britain in 1740 when the country's traditional grain crops failed and food was in short supply. Farmers planted potatoes, which had the advantage of growing in poor soil. Potatoes also contained more calories than grains. One acre (.4 ha) of potatoes yields approximately four times the calories of an acre of a grain crop. Soon, the potato became a staple in the country. The increase of potato farming made more food available, and the population dramatically increased.

This led to population growth. Food was available for more people in the country, and fewer people needed to be farmers. Those who did not have to farm to make a living could focus on producing other products. Also, there were more people to buy consumer goods. Craftspeople began producing more and distributing their products across wider regions.

By the late eighteenth century, technological advances were made in several industries. Great Britain had rich supplies of coal and iron. Scientists and inventors designed new machines and tools that could be made from iron. In turn, these machines and tools were used to manufacture products necessary for the rise of industrialization, such as textile machinery, railroad ties, and steam-engine parts. Factories opened to house the large machinery, and Great Britain's growing labor force began working in them. As factories in cities grew, people moved from the countryside to join the industrial workforce.

THE INDUSTRIAL REVOLUTION SPREADS

The Industrial Revolution began in Great Britain and spread throughout Europe. Then it spread even farther. In 1789, Slater managed to escape the attention of British officials. He disguised himself as a common laborer looking for better opportunities in the United States. With a fake name, he boarded a ship

Innovation in the Textile Industry

Before the Industrial Revolution, making cloth was time-consuming, and each piece was made one by one. Starting in 1764, however, several inventions made the textile industry more efficient. That year, inventor James Hargreaves unveiled the spinning jenny. It could spin wool into yarn with eight spindles instead of just one, as the spinning wheel did. He soon patented a spinning jenny with 16 spindles.

In 1769, Richard Arkwright invented a spinning frame, which he called a water frame. The large wooden frame with multiple rollers wove cotton faster than ever before. Powered by water, the spinning frame was completely automated. Too big for a home, it could be used only in a factory.

On the heels of Arkwright's invention, Samuel Crompton developed the mule. This machine combined the spinning jenny and the spinning frame. It produced various types of yarn, while giving workers much more control over the weaving process. The steam-powered loom, invented in 1786 by Edmund Cartwright, further increased productivity in the trade. Although many of these innovations were later improved, they originally proved that textiles could be mass-produced.

heading west across the Atlantic Ocean. Little did he know that his actions would spark the Industrial Revolution in the United States. Soon the country would experience the momentous change that had forever altered Europe. ⌐

During the Industrial Revolution, products made out of iron were in high demand.

Before the Industrial Revolution reached the United States, family members worked together on farms to make a living.

Life before the Industrial Revolution

Spanning the first colonies of the seventeenth century to the early nineteenth century, agriculture was the biggest industry in North America. During this time, people grew their own food. Farming was a way of life for most people, but it was not easy. Planting and harvesting were done by hand during the day. At night, farmers made or repaired their tools. Life revolved around the seasonal farmwork—planting in the spring and harvesting in the fall. Crops and the resulting income were directly related to a year's weather. A year of little rain could produce scarce crops, leaving just enough food for the family and little, if any, to sell. A rainy year could produce plentiful crops, allowing for the surplus to be sold. Too much rain, however, could damage crops.

Nearly everyone worked in the fields. Women and girls divided their time between farming and household chores, such as cooking and cleaning. Few shops existed, so women made their families' clothes and other essentials. Eventually, small shops opened, but many colonists still produced the items they needed at home. Early Americans excelled in craftwork, making furniture and candles for lighting their homes. Neighbors traded among themselves for handmade goods.

There were few roads, so travel by land was limited. And travel by sea was expensive. For most, making a trip to another colony meant leaving one's farm or business for days.

LAND OF OPPORTUNITY

America was rich in natural resources, such as iron and coal. There was plenty of timber, too, plus pure, fast-flowing waterways. These resources provided early colonists with the power needed to make goods. Still, only a few products were manufactured. Iron goods were made using blast furnaces. These are machines that melted down iron into a liquid. In Philadelphia, Pennsylvania, several distilleries produced rum in great quantities. Much of the alcohol was exported to England and other regions. The Chesapeake Bay area near Maryland and Virginia featured a number of the most modern flour mills of the time period.

REVOLUTIONARY WAR

In the mid-eighteenth century, the colonists in America were becoming more and more unhappy

Manufacturing Goods from Iron

Iron ore has been one of the great natural resources in the United States. By the eighteenth century, iron products were in such demand that most of the colonies began making products from iron.

Iron is a mineral that is found inside rocks, called ore. First, ore is mined. Then the iron is extracted from the ore. Blast furnaces melted the iron so it could be molded into nails, farming tools, stoves, household utensils, guns, ammunition, and more. Iron production was a good business venture. People who were willing to invest money to start an ironworks company usually made fortunes.

with the taxes imposed upon them by Great Britain. In 1775, the Revolutionary War broke out. In 1783, after eight years of fighting, the colonies finally won their independence from Great Britain.

Leaders in America began thinking about the issues facing the newly independent nation. They held differing views on the issue of industrialization: Should America remain a nation of farmers or try to become an industrial force?

Lack of industrialization had been a problem during the Revolutionary War. Once at war with Great Britain, America could no longer receive

Invention Protection

The factories of the Industrial Revolution were so productive because of their machines. The rights of those who invented the new technology needed to be protected. This was done through patents, which are documents securing a person's sole right to make or sell a product for a certain number of years.

In 1790, Congress passed the nation's first Patent Act, granting patents for up to 14 years for useful inventions. This act was replaced in 1793 with a more detailed act. The new law required a written description of the item that explained how this invention was different from anything created before it. The law also stated that a part that would improve another inventor's innovation could be patented.

In the nation's early days, some people ignored patents. They stole inventions, reproduced them, and refused to pay the inventor for the rights. Many inventors could not afford a legal battle to prevent others from making money from their stolen inventions. A similar situation occurs today with the illegal downloading of music. In that case, singers and songwriters are not paid for their work.

necessary goods from overseas. Factories were needed to make supplies—gunpowder, boots, caps, guns, and uniforms—for the Continental army. But the few, small industries could not meet America's needs and were vastly overmatched by those in Great Britain.

Opinions about Industrialization

As commander in chief of the Continental army, President George Washington had seen firsthand how detrimental a lack of factories and supplies could be. He believed the United States had to build its own factories and produce its own goods, so it would not have to depend on any other country.

Treasury Secretary Alexander Hamilton agreed with Washington. Hamilton stated that businesspeople in America could not turn their backs on industrialization. And neither could common laborers who could receive jobs in new factories. On December 5, 1791, Hamilton submitted to Congress a "Report on Manufactures." He laid out his blueprint for developing industry in the newly formed United States. Hamilton's opponents claimed that he wanted to replace agriculture with factories. But Hamilton argued that factories should never take the place of farms.

Alexander Hamilton was a strong proponent of industrialization in America.

Rather, industrialization would contribute to more effective farming methods and also build other areas of wealth.

Although industrialization brought advancements, some leaders were fearful of the negative social impact it would have in America. Major political figures such as Benjamin Franklin

Thomas Jefferson opposed industrialization in America.

and Secretary of State Thomas Jefferson did not like the grim stories they heard about health and safety issues at the mills and factories in England. Stories filtering to the United States from Great Britain told of low pay, inhumane working conditions, and terrible housing in which workers were forced to live. In 1786, Jefferson traveled to England, where he witnessed some of the poor working conditions firsthand. He was strongly opposed to bringing the same conditions to America. In Jefferson's view, it was much better to send raw materials overseas and have the British manufacture necessary goods than to make factories and their accompanying social ills part of American culture.

These leaders urged people to return to an agricultural life. But even farming was different. The self-sharpening plow that had been invented in 1785 could only be produced in a factory. Yet, some southern plantation owners did not think industrialization was necessary for a farm-based country. They had enough free slave labor to keep their plantations profitable and did not see the need to depart from traditional farming methods.

Emergence of the Two-Party System

The debate regarding industrialization was one of the factors that led to the two-party political system in the United States. Hamilton and his supporters, such as John Adams, were considered Federalists. They advocated for a strong central government, military, and financial system. Their supporters included city residents, bankers, and industrialists.

Thomas Jefferson, who was joined in his opposition to factories by James Madison and James Monroe, was a Democratic-Republican. This party advocated for rights of the state and common people. Many members of this party were farmers. Other core issues that divided the two political parties included immigration and alliances with England or France.

Slavery during the Industrial Revolution

Plantation owners in the South argued against industrialization because they had the resource of free slave labor. But once industrialization prevailed, slavery did not end. The rise of the textile industry demanded more cotton, which meant that more slaves were needed to pick cotton on plantations. Slave labor continued to contribute to the Industrial Revolution until slavery was abolished in 1865 by the Thirteenth Amendment to the U.S. Constitution.

However, industrialization won out. Soon Washington and Hamilton's point of view prevailed, and new industry and inventions were encouraged.

Southern plantation owners who made a profit using slave labor
did not think industrialization was necessary.

Samuel Slater revolutionized the textile industry in America in the late eighteenth century.

TEXTILES IN AMERICA

overnment leaders' support alone could not bring about industrialization. When Samuel Slater arrived in the United States in 1789, he brought the tools that would spark the country's industrial revolution.

Upon his arrival in New York City, Slater met Moses Brown, a New England merchant who needed help operating a textile mill. Slater offered to work for Brown. By December, Brown and Slater were partners in a project to start the country's first water-powered textile mill, located in Pawtucket, Rhode Island. Slater reconstructed the latest cloth-making machinery then in use in England. He made some adjustments to improve the equipment. After working a few years with Brown, Slater went out on his own, opening mills throughout New England.

The First Lowell Factory

Slater was not the only person who impacted the textile industry. In 1813, a group of wealthy businesspeople from Boston, Massachusetts, led by Francis Cabot Lowell, opened a textile factory along the Charles River in the village of Waltham, Massachusetts. Lowell and his partners built the first factory in America in which the entire cloth-making process—from raw cotton to finished cloth—took place under one roof. This innovation radically changed the textile industry. Lowell was able to show that his factory could produce cloth faster and cheaper than ever before.

Lowell came up with many new ideas to make his business successful. He hired New England farm girls, giving most of these young women their first opportunity to make money of their own. They were paid less than men, but they still earned more than they would have at other jobs available to them, such as seamstress work. Lowell offered the women certain extras as well, such as educational opportunities, and clean, well-run, company-owned housing that included chaperones and religious activities.

Lowell's mill also paved the way for other businesses to set up shop nearby. With the housing around the mill, shops such as

City Bound

One of the biggest changes the Industrial Revolution brought to American life was the population shift from rural to urban areas. The change was slow at first. Many country residents resisted city living. But new machinery made many farm jobs no longer necessary. Many farmhands were forced to seek work elsewhere. They went to the cities and took jobs in factories.

City living was more expensive than living in the countryside, and factory workers were not paid a great deal. They could not afford to take advantage of everything a city had to offer, such as expensive, ready-made consumer goods.

Shopping was a new experience as well. In rural areas, a general store carried a variety of items. Cities offered many stores, each carrying one type of item.

Cities were crowded, and the streets were filled with traffic. People used horse-drawn streetcars to travel around New York City and Philadelphia as early as the 1830s. At times, the wagons blocked the city streets.

bakeries, pharmacies, and bookstores opened to serve the needs of the new residents.

THE SHAREHOLDER CONCEPT

Lowell built other mills in the area as well. In order to raise money to get those mills up and running, he implemented a new idea—he sold shares of stock to the public. In other words, ordinary citizens could buy a portion of the business. When the mills profited, so did the shareholders. Other business owners began selling stock in their companies as well. The shareholder concept remains important in capitalist societies.

Lowell died in 1817. Shortly after his death, Lowell's partners moved the original Waltham mill to a small village of 200 people approximately 30 miles (48 km) north of Boston. The village later became the town of Lowell. All of its residents depended

Mining Jobs

The opening of factories and mills provided jobs in other fields. U.S. factories began using steam engines to run their operations, and those engines ran on coal. As the demand for coal went up, coal mining expanded, creating more jobs. As with many aspects of industrialization, coal mining had positive and negative aspects. The jobs provided income but under harsh and dangerous working conditions.

on the mill for their income in some form.

The Lowell Experiment, as the factory and the worker housing were called, impressed British novelist Charles Dickens. Dickens's novels tell of the horrors and abuses of factory life. Still, when he visited the factory and toured the town in 1842, he noted,

> *I cannot recall or separate one young face that gave me a painful impression; not one young girl whom, assuming it to be matter of necessity that she should gain her daily bread by labour of her hands, I would have removed from those work if I had had the power.*[1]

Company Newsletter

Workers at the first Lowell mill in Waltham wanted to make sure everyone was well informed. Workers started a magazine called the *Lowell Offering* that included articles on the latest happenings at the mill, classes being offered, and religious services being held. Today, it is common for businesses to publish company newsletters.

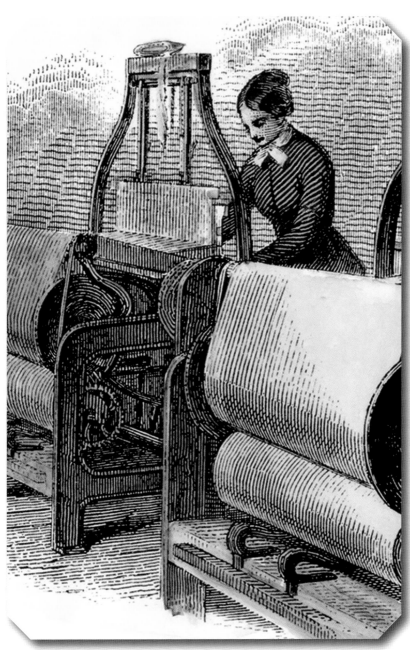

Lowell Mill Girls, as the female workers came to be called, worked for a few years before marrying and returning to domestic life.

In early America, merchants often shipped goods overseas.

TRANSPORTATION
IMPROVEMENTS

During the early stages of industrialization in America, roads were not an important means of transportation. While some roads existed in colonial times, building roads was not a priority for colonists. Because there were so few roads, it was cheaper for merchants to ship goods overseas than to transport them from state to state. Most of America's larger cities—located on the eastern seaboard—had ports, and international trading was conducted from those seaside cities.

To make industry more profitable in America, goods made in the country had to be sold within the country. That is, American-made goods had to be transported from the cities, where they were manufactured, to buyers who lived in rural areas. To accomplish this, roads had to be improved and expanded. The few roads available were coarse and rough, too poor for transporting goods. In the nation's early days, the issue of national roads had been debated in Congress, but little action was taken. Congress showed a much greater interest in building canals—human-made waterways that connected bodies of water such as rivers and lakes. The drawback to both canals and roads was the expense involved in building them. But canals had one advantage over roads: the steamboat. It could provide a cheap way to ship goods if the nation's waterways could be connected.

The first successful trial run of a steamboat occurred in 1787, when John Fitch tested his steam-powered vessel on the Delaware River. Fitch's steamboat was mechanically reliable, but it was slow and cost a great deal to build and operate.

Engineer Robert Fulton of rural Pennsylvania unveiled the submarine in 1800 and demonstrated it for Napoleon, the ruler of France. In 1807, Fulton built a faster, economically sound steamboat. He made history by turning his steamboat into a commercial success. Fulton's first steamboat, the *Clermont*, traveled from New York City to Albany, New York, in 32

Early Roads

Beginning in Virginia in 1772, early stone roads, called turnpikes, were built in America. The next turnpike, between Philadelphia and Lancaster, Pennsylvania, was completed in 1795. These were state-funded projects. Construction on federal roads lagged far behind.

During Thomas Jefferson's second term as president, from 1805 to 1809, an ongoing debate raged about building roads to link the nation from north to south and east to west. Political bickering and a high price tag blocked the project. Finally, federal legislators agreed to build one highway, known as the National Road, or the Cumberland Road.

Construction began in 1811 in Cumberland, Maryland, and the first part of the road opened in 1818. Wagons loaded with goods destined for market could be seen on the road every day. But in 1841, the project was dropped. Parts of the road built decades before were in shambles due to poor maintenance and construction. As railroad travel began to increase, the repair of these roads was left undone, as they were considered obsolete. Not until the rise of the automobile—approximately 100 years later—would roads begin to become the dominant way to travel.

Robert Fulton's Clermont *ushered in the use of steamboats for transporting goods and people.*

hours at a speed of five miles per hour (8 km). That was a relatively high speed at the time. The boat carried both people and goods. Of his steamboat, Fulton said,

It will give a cheap and quick conveyance to the merchandise on the Mississippi, Missouri and other great rivers which are now laying open their treasures to the enterprise of our countrymen. [1]

CANALS

Between 1815 and 1840, more than 3,100 miles (5,000 km) of canals were built. These waterways were dug across land to connect existing waterways, such as rivers and lakes. One of the boldest U.S. canal projects was the construction of the Erie Canal in the state of New York. The idea was to link Lake Erie in the western part of the state to the Hudson River in the east. Once the project was completed, it would open the path to what was then the great western frontier of the United States—Ohio, Michigan, Indiana, and Illinois.

In 1817, New York governor DeWitt Clinton provided $7 million

An Upstream Battle

The steamboat made a difference for southern merchants who wanted to market their goods in the North. While it had always been easy to transport goods downstream, upstream—going against the current—was another story. Before the steamboat, traveling upstream was costly and time consuming. Transportation costs were so high that many southern merchants gave up on selling to the northern markets. That all changed with the rise of timely and cost-effective steamboat transportation that could travel upstream. Northern markets were open to southern merchants, which boosted the economy in the South.

The Erie Canal allowed for goods to be shipped inland from coastal cities.

to build the original 363-mile (584-km) canal. Construction began that same year. Clinton predicted that, as a result of the canal,

> [New York City] will, in the course of time, become a granary of the world, the emporium of commerce, the seat of manufactures, the focus of great moneyed operations. And before the revolution of a century, the whole island of Manhattan, covered with inhabitants and replenished with a dense population, will constitute one vast city.[2]

The canal opened in 1825 and was an immediate success. It cost only ten dollars per ton (908 kg) to ship freight from Buffalo to New York City along the canal route, compared to $100 per ton (908 kg) by land. Goods manufactured in the East could now be affordably shipped to the Northwest. The combined canal system seemed like the best way to transport goods to market, but competition was on the way.

STEAM-POWERED LOCOMOTIVES

Steam could also be used to power transportation on land. Wealthy inventor John Stevens of New Jersey, who built several steamboats, wanted to try the steam engine on railroad tracks. Stevens received North America's first railroad charter, or rights to build a railroad, in 1815. Stevens built the first steam-powered locomotive in 1825 and demonstrated it in New Jersey. Interest grew, and

Taking a Toll

The Erie Canal was paid for by tolls. It took only nine years for the tolls to cover the entire cost of the engineering marvel. When the canal was first completed, it was called the Eighth Wonder of the World. Some states found ways other than tolls to pay for their canals, including taxes.

soon he and others obtained federal grants to start laying the groundwork for a U.S. railway system.

Giant steam-powered locomotives would soon be able to haul more people and goods than steamboats—and at a lower cost. A railway system came one step closer to reality when, in 1830, New York inventor Peter Cooper unveiled the first U.S.-built steam locomotive for public use, called the Tom Thumb.

There were still some obstacles to overcome, however. The railroad spikes that held tracks in place would often come loose, shifting the tracks. Trains would then jump the tracks. The tracks would give off sparks, which started brush fires. These problems made the public and investors skeptical about trains as a reliable form of mass transportation. The problems were fixed by building better and stronger track beds, which then encouraged more railroad construction. By 1852, the United States had approximately 12,600 miles (19,312 km) of track, including a railway from New York City to New Orleans, Louisiana.

Building track was difficult, time-consuming labor done mostly by hand. While approximately 29,000 miles (46,671 km) of track had been constructed by 1861, railroad building increased following the American Civil War. Before the war, track was being constructed in the East and in the West, but the tracks did not connect at any point. Also, there was no standard for the width of rails—some tracks were wider and some were narrower. Many railroad tracks could not link together. It was not until the 1880s that a standard width was set, and railroads that did not meet the standard were fixed to match.

Before this, a large railroad project was started. In 1863, work began on a transcontinental railroad. The new line would link the compatible network of tracks in the eastern United States, which already reached the Mississippi River, with the West Coast.

The Union Pacific Railroad was building track westward from Council Bluffs, Iowa. The Central Pacific

Gelatin Dessert

Peter Cooper, the inventor of the Tom Thumb locomotive, also invented the first gelatin dessert, but he never promoted it. He sold the 1845 patent for the fun, wobbly dessert to cough syrup manufacturer Pearl B. Wait in 1895. Wait packaged the dessert and changed the name from gelatin to Jell-O, the popular fruity treat.

The last rail for the transcontinental railroad was laid
on May 10, 1869, in Promontory, Utah.

Railroad was laying track eastward from Sacramento,
California. The Central Pacific portion of the tracks
had to cross the Sierra Nevada Mountains in order to
reach Nevada and then Promontory, Utah, where the
tracks would meet.

A Huge Engineering Feat

The transcontinental railroad is considered one
of the greatest engineering feats of the nineteenth
century. As soon as it was completed in 1869, it

made wagon trains and stagecoaches obsolete. People could safely travel across the country by train in seven days. It took four to six months to make the same trip by wagon, and travelers had to contend with disease, outlaws, rainstorms, and heavy winds along the trail.

Waterways presented serious obstacles to the expansion of trains. The transcontinental railroad was not a direct link to the East Coast until 1872, when the Union Pacific Missouri River Bridge opened. Before that, the trains crossed the Missouri River by ferry.

The railroad was a much cheaper and faster form of transportation for people and goods than steamships had been. While the transcontinental railroad was being built, other smaller railroads were linking to it. Convenient and economical transportation, so necessary to the success of the U.S. Industrial Revolution, was becoming a reality.

Once the transcontinental railroad was complete, cross-country trips were safer, cheaper, and faster.

After the Civil War, Southern states began opening factories to improve their ruined economies.

BIG BUSINESS

In 1865, the American Civil War ended. The industrialization that had occurred in the North played a major role in the war's conclusion. While the South's economy was focused on plantations worked by slaves, the North held the vast majority of the country's factories and workers. This contributed to wartime production, which included weapons. It meant the North could build rail lines to transport soldiers to battle. Northern factories were booming during the Civil War and continued to do so once the war ended. Many areas of the South were destroyed during the war; machines and factories were needed to help rebuild that area of the country.

Wrapped and Ready

During the Civil War, food for the Northern troops was being prepared in a new way—it was canned and packaged. This way, the troops could carry the food with them and eat whenever they wanted. After the war, packaged food became available to the public. Food companies found ways to make the packaging attractive to appeal to the customers.

With the ongoing improvements in transportation, northern factories were able to ship their goods easily to faraway, southern markets. The growing demand for manufactured goods, such as clothing and shoes, led to the opening of more small factories.

The Rise of Big Business

Competition among factories drove the prices of consumer goods down, which was good for customers. Several factory owners found ways to outdo their competition by buying raw materials in large quantities. Sellers offered discounts to those who bought in bulk, so the owners' costs were reduced. This allowed owners to expand their factories, add more equipment and workers, produce more goods, fill larger orders, and meet increasing demand faster. Expanding a factory required the input of additional money, but the factory owners soon made the money back with the added business. Smaller factory operations that did not have the money to expand often could not keep up with larger factories. They went out of business.

As this happened time and again, competition gradually reduced. With fewer competitors, large companies were free to raise prices—they did not have to worry as much that buyers would take their business elsewhere. Often, prices became higher than they had been before.

If a small factory did survive, it barely scraped by. The larger factories with better equipment often bought out their smaller competitors. These buyouts created huge businesses. In turn, the giant companies purchased the latest technology, acquired large quantities of raw materials, and hired even more workers. Expansion allowed the companies to combine many aspects of production, which had been spread out among different companies, under

During the late nineteenth century, more and larger factories opened across the United States.

one company name. And with better transportation, these businesses opened plants in other parts of the country, increasing their customer base. The General Electric Company was formed in 1892 after two smaller electrical equipment companies combined. The company continued to expand and took over a large share of the electric industry.

Monopolies

Andrew Carnegie is one of the most well-known business owners of this time. Though he made money in a number of areas, the Scottish immigrant made his name and most of his fortune in the steel industry. In 1875, Carnegie opened his first steel mill in Braddock, Pennsylvania. Eventually, the Carnegie Steel Company had mills around the country. They produced steel using the Bessemer process, which converted iron into steel. This allowed the company to produce steel faster and more economically than any of its competitors. The company sold much of its steel to railroads and construction companies. Most of New York City's elevated railway tracks were made with Carnegie steel. So was the Brooklyn Bridge.

Carnegie built a self-reliant business, and it soon became a monopoly. This is a business that has exclusive control of an industry. Carnegie controlled everything relating to steel, including the companies that supplied his plants with the raw materials to make it. He controlled even the coal to run the furnaces in his plants. During the Industrial Revolution, Carnegie and businesspeople like him built what are called vertical monopolies:

Andrew Carnegie built the Carnegie Steel Company as a vertical monopoly.

they owned every company that had anything to do with producing and delivering their goods.

Carnegie could ship his steel more cheaply than anyone else because he controlled the railroad that shipped it. He would buy out steel companies that could not compete with his and gain an even bigger share of the steel market. By 1900, Carnegie's steel mills made a yearly profit of $40 million.

By 1901, however, the steel magnate had grown weary of the business, and he decided to sell. He turned to wealthy banker J. P. Morgan, who owned United States Steel Corporation. Carnegie sold his entire share of his business to Morgan for $480 million—approximately $12.5 billion today. That made Carnegie the richest man in the United States at the time.

Morgan was among a handful of individuals who could single-handedly control an entire industry. Sugar and tobacco were two industries bought out by such wealthy men. The businessmen would pay for new technology to make products less expensively and then buy out all competitors. The result of a buyout of all companies selling a similar product is known as a horizontal monopoly. These industrialists could then control a product's price as well as the wages paid to workers in the factories producing the product.

John D. Rockefeller and his brother, William, bought into an oil pipeline in 1865. They set up the Standard Oil Company of Ohio in 1870. By 1879, the company had gained control of 90 percent of the country's oil refineries through a series of business deals and mergers.

THE DOWNSIDE OF BIG BUSINESS

Monopolies posed a great threat to the welfare of the nation. They gave control over the marketplace and jobs to a mighty few. This forced smaller businesses to fail, prevented competing businesses from starting up, and limited the opportunities for most Americans. Many of those who ran the monopolies abused workers, kept wages low, and created unhealthy and unsafe workplaces.

Many U.S. government officials worried about the effect

Theodore Roosevelt: Trust Buster

President Theodore Roosevelt served as president of the United States from 1901 to 1909. He contributed greatly to the era of industrialization in the country. Roosevelt approved construction of the Panama Canal, the waterway that greatly expanded U.S. trade. He also fought hard against monopolies. He believed they stood in the way of new ideas and inventions and led to unfair business and labor practices. In his view, the businessmen who ran them were ruthless and uncaring. Roosevelt recognized government's failure at keeping these businesses in check:

The power of the mighty industrial overlords of the country had increased with giant strides, while the methods of controlling them, or checking abuses by them on the part of the people, through the Government, remained archaic and therefore practically impotent.[1]

With the passing of the Sherman Antitrust Act, Roosevelt worked hard to break up monopolies that were stifling economic competition. In addition to oil, he also split up railroad and tobacco trusts, which are conglomerations similar to monopolies. So many monopolies were dismantled during his administration, in fact, that people called him the "trust buster."

of monopolies on the nation's economy. In 1890, Congress passed the Sherman Antitrust Act. That made it illegal for any merger to occur if the move would limit or control an industry. Under that law, action was taken against Rockefeller's Standard Oil Company. In March 1892, the Ohio Supreme Court found that Standard Oil Company was indeed a monopoly and ordered that it be broken up. To avoid the breakup, Rockefeller reorganized the company and moved it to New Jersey.

Under the leadership of President Theodore Roosevelt, the U.S. attorney general's office brought 44 lawsuits against monopolies, including those run by Morgan and Rockefeller. Some of the cases went to the U.S. Supreme Court, and many of the monopolies were eventually broken up. Standard Oil Company, for instance, became 34 smaller companies in 1911.

This cartoon shows how monopolies such as the Standard Oil Company disregarded the interests of regular citizens.

Crowds of people gathered at the Centennial Exhibition in 1876 to view the many inventions and new technologies on display.

AMERICAN INGENUITY

Propelled by the Industrial Revolution, the United States developed into an industrial superpower. The nation's industrial strength was celebrated at the Centennial Exhibition, held in Philadelphia, Pennsylvania, in 1876.

The event showcased thousands of amazing inventions, drawing more than 9 million people over a period of five months. So many U.S. inventors wanted to display their time- and labor-saving inventions that it took 250 buildings on the 285-acre (115 ha) fairgrounds to house all of them. Inventors from foreign countries also displayed their latest work for the curious crowds.

The fair attracted a great deal of news coverage. The press ran stories about new machines that made everything from shoes to envelopes. Among the inventions were gadgets for the home, including gas-powered cooking stoves and refrigeration devices that kept food from spoiling. New printing machines were displayed, as were typewriters and sewing machines.

Farmers could see the latest innovations in agricultural equipment. At the F. and J. Heinz Company booth, people were invited to taste a new product called ketchup. Root beer was also introduced at the fair. The Centennial Exhibition gave people a glimpse into the future of technology. It also served as a reminder of the nation's fast-paced industrialization and was billed as a salute to U.S. accomplishments.

SCENES IN COTTON LAND.—THE COTTON-GIN.—SEE PAGE 55.

Eli Whitney's cotton gin made cleaning cotton a much quicker task. This allowed for more cotton to be grown and sold in the country.

THE COTTON GIN AND INTERCHANGEABLE PARTS

Inventions such as Eli Whitney's cotton gin in 1793 had thrust the United States at full speed into the Industrial Revolution. As a young man, Whitney witnessed the difficult process of pulling seeds out of freshly picked cotton by hand. It took a person an entire day to pick seeds from just one pound (0.5 kg) of cotton. His machine could pull the seeds out of 50 pounds (23 kg) of cotton a day.

Whitney's next innovation was interchangeable parts, which he first used in guns. Identical parts could replace each other in manufactured products. For example, a broken part in one gun could be replaced by an identical part from another gun of the same model. Until that time, every gun had been custom made by a gunsmith, so no two guns were identical. If a gun broke, an expert gunsmith would have to make custom parts to repair the gun or the weapon would be useless. This was a very time-consuming process and made guns costly to craft. Interchangeable parts became an invaluable factor for the development of mass production.

ELECTRICITY AND MORE

Another invention that revolutionized industry was the practical lightbulb, invented by Thomas Edison in 1879. Among his many inventions, Edison developed

The Best Part

Eli Whitney's concept of interchangeable parts became known as the "American system." Interchangeable parts, still a backbone of manufacturing, would have a much more lasting impact on U.S. life than his cotton gin. Interchangeable parts would become standard for producing many different products throughout the world for years to come. These items included clocks, watches, farm tools, sewing machines, bicycles, and cars.

Thomas Edison developed the practical lightbulb and electric power plants, which soon changed how people lit their homes and businesses.

an electrical grid large enough to power entire cities. He also built electric power plants all over the United States. Considered one of the greatest inventors of all time, Edison had 1,093 patents to his name in the United States. He also held patents in France, England, and Germany.

As a young man, Edison moved to New York City and got a job as a telegraph operator. In his spare time, the young inventor developed a better ticker-tape machine. This recorded stock prices and kept stockbrokers informed of the latest price changes. He sold the invention for $40,000 in 1869, which is the equivalent of approximately $650,000 today.

With the success of his ticker-tape machine, Edison turned to inventing full time. He is credited with opening the first industrial research laboratory in the world in 1876 in Menlo Park, New Jersey. In that lab, Edison developed some of his most renowned inventions, including the phonograph, similar to a record player, and the motion picture camera.

AN EQUAL OPPORTUNITY PURSUIT

For most of the United States' first 100 years, men received the most credit for life-changing innovations. Among these male inventors were

Lighting the Way

Before Thomas Edison perfected the practical lightbulb, homes were lit using coal gas. This method was dirty and left a black sooty residue in the house. The gas often caused fires and polluted the air. It took Edison more than 3,000 tries before he came up with a practical working lightbulb. Despite all the failures along the way, Edison never gave up. He always envisioned how simple it would be to light homes and businesses if his bulb were to become a reality.

Cyrus McCormick, who invented the reaper; John Deere, developer of the steel plow; Elias Howe, who first patented the sewing machine; Linus Yale Jr., inventor of the cylinder lock; Elisha Graves Otis, creator of the elevator; and, of course, Edison.

But women also made significant contributions to the U.S. Industrial Revolution. Sarah Mather invented a telescope and a lamp in 1845 that let sea vessels explore the ocean depths. Martha Coston perfected and patented pyrotechnic flares, also known as night signals. These allowed ships to set up a communications system that saved lives and won military battles. In addition to creating cookbooks, Fannie Farmer introduced science into the kitchen by establishing a standardized measuring system.

Margaret Knight developed the safety device that was used in textile mills to stop machinery if a worker got too close to it. This device drastically reduced the number of accidents in the mills, preventing workplace injuries and keeping employees on the job. Knight was one of the most productive female inventors of the nineteenth century, amassing 27 patents.

Women also invented kitchen tools, apparel, and cookware. While only 35 women were granted patents between 1809 and 1850, that number jumped to 859 by 1876. Despite their success as inventors, women were to be excluded from the 1876 Centennial Exhibition. But they made an aggressive push to have a presence there and succeeded—even though they were not given space in the buildings alongside male inventors. Nevertheless, 79 women gathered in their own building to display the fruits of their work.

Many fairgoers were overwhelmed by the sheer creativity of these women. Elizabeth Duane Gillespie, the head of the Women's Centennial Committee, said the point of the women's pavilion at the exhibition was to:

> give to the mass of women who were laboring by the needle and obtaining only a scanty subsistence, the opportunity to see what women were capable of attaining . . . in other and higher branches of industry.[1]

In the Bag

Though best known for her stop-motion device, Margaret Knight also has the distinction of inventing the machine that makes the flat-bottomed, brown paper bag. She invented the machine in 1868 and opened her own company, the Eastern Paper Bag Company, in 1870. Her design is still used to make paper bags.

African-American Inventors

While women presented their inventions at the Centennial Exhibition, African Americans were mostly overlooked, despite the fact that many African Americans made meaningful contributions. In 1872, African-American engineer Elijah McCoy invented the automatic lubricator used to keep car, truck, and train axels running smoothly. Factories and mechanics who used the device felt it was the best lubricator ever made. They refused to accept a substitute, even though some inventors tried to

---

Life as an Inventor

The life of an inventor in the early days of the United States was not easy. Inventing was an expensive and time-consuming undertaking. Inventors had to pay for all their materials themselves. They often spent years perfecting single inventions because they failed time and again. Most of these creative people put all the money they had into their work. Some lived in poverty, investing all their resources in an invention they felt would eventually make them rich. While Elias Howe worked on the sewing machine, he, his wife, and their three children were practically destitute. Many inventors used their homes as their workshops. Charles Goodyear invented vulcanized rubber, which is used for car tires, on his kitchen stove.

Some inventions took years to catch on. Howe had to wait four years before buyers became interested in his sewing machine. Others never found a market. Also, unscrupulous people often tried to steal the idea behind a successful invention and sell it as their own. That led to costly and lengthy lawsuits over patent rights. Eli Whitney nearly went bankrupt fighting over patent rights for his cotton gin. For most inventors, it took fierce determination to stay the course, and that attitude became a hallmark of American ingenuity.

pass off their designs as McCoy's. Those buying the McCoy lubricator would ask the seller, "Is this the real McCoy?" Hence the famous saying was coined.

African-American inventor Norbert Rillieux developed the multiple-effect vacuum evaporator in 1843. This device, which revolutionized sugar processing, also helped make condensed milk, soaps, and glue. Henry Blair developed a seed planter for corn in 1834 and a corn harvester two years later. His inventions made farming much more efficient. Although not displayed at the Centennial Exhibition, these and other inventions by African Americans were highly successful in the marketplace.

THE WORLD'S COLUMBIAN EXPOSITION

Inventions by African Americans did not receive much attention at the 1893 World's Columbian Exposition in Chicago, Illinois, either. As before, though, women inventors were able to secure their own building at the fair. The World's Columbian Exposition held many notable attractions, including one exhibition building devoted solely to electrical devices and the world's first Ferris wheel. Originally known as the Chicago wheel, the 264-foot (80-meter) high amusement ride was built to rival the Eiffel Tower, the centerpiece of the Paris Exposition held four years earlier. Designed by bridge builder George Ferris Jr., the Chicago wheel got its power from two steam engines. The wheel had 36 cars, and it could make one nonstop revolution in nine minutes. The world had never seen anything like it. As a credit to the man who built it, awestruck fairgoers referred to the attraction as the Ferris wheel.

The Centennial Exhibition in Philadelphia, the World's Columbian Exposition, and other fairs around the world displayed some of the greatest inventions of the Industrial Revolution. However, the best inventions were yet to come. Beginning in the early twentieth century, these would change transportation more dramatically than ever before.

Transportation Advances

Orville and Wilbur Wright developed the first airplane and took their maiden flight in 1903. Once the Wright brothers got off the ground, they made many improvements to their flying machine between 1903 and 1905. They overcame a major obstacle by building a lightweight engine that was strong enough to power their flying machine but not weigh it down.

In 1903, Henry Ford opened an automobile factory in Michigan. He was determined to make a car everyone could afford. Five years later, Ford came out with the Model T. The Model T had a price tag of $850—expensive but cheaper than the luxurious Packard, which sold for more than $2,000. Ford implemented the assembly-line process in 1913. An assembly line allowed workers to stay in one location and carry out one specific task in the car-manufacturing process. By using an assembly line, Ford made the Model T much less expensive. By 1924, the price for each car was only $290. The assembly-line process, which is still used today, kept costs low enough so that more than 15 million Model Ts were on the road by 1927.

Throughout the Industrial Revolution, men and women came up with numerous inventions

The Wright Airplane

One of the Wright brothers' early contracts for their flying machine was with the U.S. Army. But the military required the Wrights' invention to contain two seats instead of the original one. The brothers agreed to develop the two-seat flying machine.

that changed the face of many U.S. industries.
Another industry greatly affected was the field of
communication. ⌐

Henry Ford's development of the assembly line
revolutionized manufacturing.

*Before new technology, people communicated by sending letters.
One mail service used was the Pony Express.*

THE COMMUNICATIONS BOOM

At the dawn of the U.S. Industrial Revolution in the late eighteenth century, letters were the only way to send messages. It took weeks for letters to travel from one part of the country to another. In the nineteenth century,

several new inventions increased the speed and
reliability of communication.

The Telegraph

A personal tragedy sparked the beginning
of faster and more reliable communications
technology. In 1825, Samuel Morse, a 35-year-
old artist, traveled from his home in New Haven,
Connecticut, to Washington DC to paint a portrait
of the Marquis de Lafayette. Several months into the
project, Morse received a handwritten note from
his father, delivered by a messenger on horseback,
stating that Morse's wife was dead. Morse returned
home immediately, but by the time he got there, his
wife had been buried. The heartbroken artist was
determined to find a quicker way to send and receive
long-distance messages.

For several years, Morse considered various
ideas. But he did not come up with a workable plan
until he met Charles Thomas Jackson in 1832. A
scientist, Jackson introduced Morse to the concept
of electromagnetism, which produces an electric
field, or charge. Jackson's theory was simple:
Electrical impulses can be carried along wires for
long distances. Morse would use that concept as a

springboard for his invention. He reasoned, "If the presence of electricity can be made visible in any part of the circuit, I see no reason why intelligence may not be transmitted instantaneously by electricity."[1]

Morse formulated his idea for the single-wire telegraph in 1832, but it took several more years before he developed a working model. Between 1832 and 1837, Morse developed a prototype of the telegraph. In 1838, he created a character code of dots and dashes to represent letters and numbers so messages could be sent in the form of electrical pulses. Morse then needed to convince Congress that it was worth spending money to wire the country so the telegraph system could be put in place. After several failed attempts, Morse finally won over Congress in 1843. The legislators agreed to spend $30,000 to assemble wires for use by Morse's telegraph.

On May 24, 1844, Morse proved that the telegraph worked by sending a message from Washington DC to Baltimore, Maryland. Two years later, private companies were constructing telegraph lines throughout the country. By 1851, Mississippi Valley Printing Telegraph Company, which would become Western Union Telegraph Company in 1856, was in operation.

The speed of the new communications technology appealed to many Americans. But some were suspicious of the new devices because messages could no longer be kept private. Telegraph operators at both the sending and the receiving ends of a message could read the correspondence.

Setting aside those concerns, bank managers, law enforcement officers, military leaders, and even government officials used the telegraph in place of letters to communicate more quickly. Up until 1876, sending a telegram was the fastest way to

The End of the Pony Express

For 18 months, between April 1860 and October 1861, the Pony Express offered the fastest and most direct communication between California and the rest of the United States, which extended only as far west as Missouri. Young, strong cowboys riding well-conditioned horses took mail across a 1,800-mile (2,897-km) route between St. Joseph, Missouri, and Sacramento, California, in ten days or fewer. In 1860, overland mail by stagecoach took more than 20 days.

During the months the Pony Express was in operation, inventors worked to link the East and the West with telegraph lines. After Samuel Morse proved in 1844 that the telegraph could work, the technology grew on the East Coast. The next great frontier was connecting East and West. On October 24, 1861, the first transcontinental telegraph established almost instantaneous communication between the eastern and western parts of the United States. The Pony Express became obsolete. The mail service went out of business two days after the first telegraph message was sent and received.

Many people worked at the Western Union Telegraph Company, which grew with the spread of the telegraph.

communicate. A good telegraph operator could tap 25 to 40 words per minute.

As the telegraph business boomed, inventors worked on a way for people to use wires to hear each other's voices. If one of these inventors had a breakthrough, this yet-to-be-named device would completely change the way Americans communicated.

The Telephone

Like Morse, Alexander Graham Bell pursued his work as an inventor because of a personal passion. Bell was born in Edinburgh, Scotland, in 1847. He had always had an interest in speech, since his grandfather and his father worked extensively on elocution, the art of public speaking. Bell was especially close with his mother, who was deaf. Because of this, he became interested in inventing hearing devices when he was only 12 years old.

Bell moved to Boston in 1871 when he received a teaching job at Boston University. There he met other inventors. Determined to do away with deafness, Bell worked on creating hearing devices. He also became convinced that he could develop acoustic telegraphy—a way to transmit voice over telegraph lines. While Bell found people willing to back his project financially, he realized that he did not have enough knowledge to make his idea a reality.

In 1874, Bell met Thomas Watson, an electrical designer and mechanic at a local Boston machine

Wired

By 1865, the telegraph was the most important means of communication in the nation. More than 83,000 miles (133,500 km) of wire carried messages all over the country from private citizens and businesses alike. The telegraph was also responsible for delivering breaking news to newspapers, which, in turn, printed stories about the events.

shop. Watson was intrigued by Bell's concept of acoustic telegraphy and agreed to work with him. On March 10, 1876, Bell spoke the famous words through his sound telegraphy device: "Mr. Watson. Come here. I want to see you."[2] Later that year, Bell and his partners offered to sell their revolutionary device to Western Union for $100,000. Western Union President William Orton declined the offer. He said that while the device was a good novelty item, "What use could this company make of an electrical toy?"[3]

Undeterred, Bell founded the Bell Telephone Company in 1877. Within two years, his patent on the telephone was worth at least $1 million. The telephone industry provided jobs for thousands of people across the United States and boosted commerce throughout the world. It was not long before the telephone was considered a necessity, rather than a luxury, for a business. It took a few more years before the price of telephones and telephone service

Telephone Operators

When the telephone was first invented, all calls had to be placed through an operator. To save money, the newly formed Bell Telephone Company hired teenage boys for the job. Many of the boys already had worked as telegraph operators, so they seemed like natural candidates. However, the boys were rude to customers. In response, the phone company changed its policy and decided to hire women instead. In 1878, Emma Nutt became the first female telephone operator. Once women replaced all the boys, it took decades (until the 1960s) for males to get another chance at the operator's board.

decreased enough to be affordable for the general public.

Together, the invention of the telegraph and the telephone created many jobs. In addition, inventions that were part of the U.S. Industrial Revolution, such as gas-powered stoves and electric sewing machines, helped make household chores easier. They gave women—especially single women—a chance to work outside the home. The female workforce increased dramatically between 1880 and 1890. Women now possessed more spending money, becoming consumers with buying power.

From the Comfort of Home

Like any business, the Bell Telephone Company had to attract customers when it first started. The company came up with an advertising campaign telling how the telephone would make people's lives easier. Alexander Graham Bell figured that men had more money than women, so he geared the ad campaign to men. He explained that if a man had a phone in his house, his wife could order dinner right from home, the doctor was just a phone call away, and so was his best friend—provided, of course, that all these people had phones as well.

PUBLISHING

Another means of communication was greatly enhanced by the U.S. Industrial Revolution as well. Newspapers and other kinds of publishing underwent tremendous technological advancements in the nineteenth century. Steam-powered printing presses replaced manually run presses. The rotary press, invented by Richard Hoe in 1843, made it possible to print images on rolls of paper, rather than individual sheets. The linotype machine, with its keyboard to type words, replaced manual typesetting. Before this, workers had to place each letter by hand. These devices made printing newspapers faster and cheaper.

Technological improvements in publishing also brought down the cost of producing magazines and books. Mass production and distribution of printed materials became possible. Both the number of publishing companies and the number of published items increased. For example, in 1850, approximately 2,500 different newspapers were printed in the United States. By 1880, there were more than 11,000.

The First Phone Book

New Haven, Connecticut, was the first city to print a telephone directory. The book of phone users was published in 1879. It listed the names of 50 people who had phones in their homes or businesses. But the book did not contain any telephone numbers because all calls at the time had to be placed through an operator.

Many women worked as telephone operators
once the device took hold across the country.

Negative aspects of the Industrial Revolution included low pay, crowded factories, unsafe equipment, and long hours.

WORKING CONDITIONS

he Industrial Revolution had a major impact, both positive and negative, on the lives of workers in the United States. Before it began, strict working hours and break times did not control farmers. While they were governed by the seasons and the weather, farmers still worked at their own pace. They took breaks when they wanted or needed to. For the most part, they were their own bosses, and many of the people who worked for them were family members. Once the economy shifted, workers' lives were never the same.

Factory Jobs

When industrialization first began in the United States, a great number of workers flocked to cities to work in textile mills. For the first time, they worked to make a profit for someone else. Managers decided when they started work, when they took breaks, and when their shifts ended. Factory workers were told what they could and could not do. They could be fired for simply talking to another employee while on the job.

In order to attract workers, factory owners offered incentives, such as housing close to the mill or free educational courses. But these were outweighed by negative aspects. The workers were not paid very much and worked long hours. Most were women and children, who were relatively powerless compared to men, and so could be paid less. Workers complained about the poor conditions, but factory owners avoided having to address the problem by having a changing workforce. Most of the women employees were saving money to get married or to assist their families. When they accomplished their goal, they left. So even those who endured the difficulties usually did not stay on the job very long.

More Workers, Worse Conditions

By the 1840s, more factories opened and made many kinds of goods. The full U.S. workforce had changed from mostly men to a mix of men and women. Some factory workers were immigrants. They came looking for better opportunities than were available to them in their countries of origin. In the case of Irish workers, they were fleeing a famine, or mass starvation, in their homeland.

In the early nineteenth century, the United States did not have enough workers. Companies actively encouraged people from other parts of the world, especially Europe, to come to America. It was a land with bountiful opportunities. As immigrants flowed into the nation, workers became plentiful. Many of the immigrants were unskilled and provided cheap labor. Factory owners were not interested in employee grievances, such as low pay. The owners could afford to replace unhappy workers with the many people who were looking for any jobs at all, even dangerous jobs that did not pay well.

The factory environment was both unsafe and unhealthy. Few, if any, safety precautions were taken. Machinery used during the Industrial Revolution had sharp edges and hot surfaces. Machinery was designed to operate at high speeds with split-second rotating, churning, and high-pressure action. The equipment did not shut off if a person's clothing

The Triangle Shirtwaist Fire

A devastating fire at the Triangle Shirtwaist Company in New York City on March 25, 1911, illustrated what could happen when work-place health and safety issues were ignored. The company manufactured women's blouses, called shirtwaists.

The fire started around 4:40 p.m. in the ten-story Asch Building, which housed Triangle's 500 employees—mostly women, some as young as 14. There had been complaints about the working conditions in the factory for years. Flammable fabrics and fabric scraps littered the workplace. In addition, open gas pilot lights were used for lighting, workers smoked on the job, and exit doors were locked to keep work-ers from taking breaks. Nothing was ever done about the complaints.

When the fire broke out, many of the work-ers on the ninth floor could not get out of the building because of the locked doors. The building's one fire escape collapsed. The blaze caused the deaths of 146 workers. Many of them died when they jumped out of windows to escape the blaze. Others died as a result of smoke inhalation inside the building. The tragic fire led to the passage of important workplace safety legislation in the state of New York.

or limbs became caught in it. The long shifts ranged from 12 to 14 hours and caused employee fatigue that contributed to workplace accidents. Employee injuries and fatalities were considered part of the cost of doing business. If employees could not work after being hurt on the job, they were simply replaced.

As larger and more powerful machinery was invented to increase production, the noise levels inside factories became deafening. No protective gear was provided to prevent employees from suffering hearing loss or unbearable headaches. Lighting and ventilation in the factories were also extremely poor. With an endless stream of immigrants coming to the United States looking for jobs, there was no shortage of people seeking factory work, so factory owners could afford to set their own rules. No governmental regulatory codes were in place to protect the safety of workers.

Some factory workers were not paid by the hour. Instead, they were paid according to the amount of work they completed. For instance, in the textile industry, workers were paid by how many pieces of clothing they made. Being paid this way added pressure to already strained workers. Working long hours in unhealthy working conditions and for little pay, textile workers began calling their workplaces "sweatshops."

THE MEATPACKING INDUSTRY

One area that showed both the incredible advancements and the horrifying labor conditions of the Industrial Revolution was the meatpacking industry. Chicago was at the center of the industry. By 1890, approximately 25,000 workers slaughtered 14 million animals each year. The meatpacking industry benefited from numerous innovations. They included refrigeration, machines that allowed for slaughtering many animals at once, and more railroad tracks that allowed for transporting the livestock.

While business boomed, however, employees suffered. Individual butchers needed training and skill to do their jobs. In the meatpacking plants, an employee was just one part of a large assembly line that slaughtered animals and readied

Hard Work Is Good for the Soul

Factory owners argued that hard work was good for the soul. They often used the argument to justify forcing their employees to work from 12 to 14 hours a day and in extreme instances, from 16 to 18 hours a day. Throughout the 1880s, many workers pushed for a ten-hour workday, and a few factory owners gave in to the demand. But most employers claimed that the long, hard days were good for workers.

Meatpacking employees worked on fast assembly lines with sharp equipment; workplace injuries were common.

them for sale. Employees needed little knowledge to perform the unskilled labor. They were forced to work as quickly as possible, thereby making more money for the company. Unfortunately, knives and machinery were dangerous, and more accidents occurred the faster the assembly line moved.

Manufacturers also increased their profits by paying employees low wages and forcing them to work more than eight hours each day. The average hourly wage ranged from 16¢ to 18¢—equivalent to approximately $3.90 to $4.40 an hour today. Most women and children earned less than men for the same work.

LABOR UNREST

Meanwhile, the prices of goods fell. Yet many consumers—the people who worked in the factories making the goods—could not afford to buy them. As early as the 1830s, labor activists were complaining about the low pay and long hours. They began organizing strikes. During a strike, workers stopped going to work, in protest of an aspect of their jobs that they wanted changed. Strikes halted the manufacturing of goods at factories. Workers hoped this would force owners to meet their demands, which usually included safer working conditions or better pay.

Unions began to form. These organized worker groups sought better working conditions. The National Trades Union (NTU), founded in 1834, was the first national union, but there were some smaller unions, too. More than 300,000 people belonged to unions in the 1830s. Then, an

Mother Jones: Labor Crusader

Mary Harris Jones lost her husband and four children to yellow fever in 1867, when the family lived in Tennessee. She knew about the terrible working conditions in the factories from her husband, who had been an ironworker.

With her family gone, Mother Jones, as she came to be known, took up the plight of U.S. workers in the 1870s. She traveled around the country well into her eighties. She organized unions, exposed terrible working conditions, and fought for workers' rights. "My address is like my shoes. It travels with me. I [live] where there is a fight against wrong," Mother Jones was fond of saying.[1] She helped found the Industrial Workers of the World, a labor union, in 1905.

economic downturn in the United States in 1837 caused a lack of jobs. People worried that there was not enough work to go around. They became hesitant to demand better working conditions. As a result, the NTU folded in 1837. However, it set the stage for other unions to rise in later years. Those significant groups included the National Labor Union in 1866, the Noble Order of the Knights of Labor in 1869, and the American Federation of Labor in 1886.

Local unions soon began to return. Factory owners fought these unions in court, and some judges ruled that the unions were illegal. Owners fired union leaders. They made new employees sign agreements that they would not join unions. The agreements also stated that the union did not speak for all workers and so could not make deals on their behalf. Still unions protested for better workplace conditions. Between 1881 and 1890, more than 24,000 strikes occurred. Miners and factory and railroad workers walked off their jobs. At times, violence broke out when strikers clashed with police or factory officials who tried to end the strike.

In 1892, employees at Andrew Carnegie's steel plant in Homestead, Pennsylvania, went on strike. They were protesting the lowering of wages and attempts to shut down their labor union. Tensions rose. Twelve people died in the violence that broke out between the strikers and the manufacturers.

Poverty Wages

According to the U.S. Census Bureau, in 1890, the average family of four had an annual income of $380. That was well below the poverty level, which was set by the bureau at $530 a year for a family of four. Employers said they had good, moral reasons for keeping wages low. Doing so kept the working class from spending money on alcohol or gambling, they argued. In their view, it also allowed employers to share the wealth by hiring more workers.

ADVANCES FOR LABOR

Labor unions in the twentieth century made great advances on behalf of their members. They did so by using collective bargaining. When a problem arose, they began by bringing it up with management. If a deal could not be worked out, they went on strike. Sometimes unions used violence, as in the strike in Homestead, to get their points heard.

Easy Targets

Factory owners took advantage of children, especially during times when adults were making demands for better pay, hours, and working conditions. Children were afraid of their bosses. Their fear alone kept them from organizing any type of work stoppage. Curious children would innocently play without supervision near dangerous machines. They could easily be mangled if the equipment suddenly started running. Overworked, tired children were also more vulnerable to disease, especially in the filthy factory environments.

Unions also pressured Congress to make new laws protecting workers from abuses. Among the laws that passed were those improving workers' compensation. Others included safer job sites, overtime pay, health benefits, minimum wage laws, paid vacations and holidays, unemployment benefits, and grievance proceedings.

The Fair Labor Standards Act, passed by Congress in 1938, set the workweek at 40 hours. It also made child labor illegal. Now children under 16 years old could not work in factories at all; those under the age of 18 were banned from performing certain dangerous jobs. New laws also made it mandatory for children to attend school, which helped curb abuses of children in the workplace.

During the Homestead Strike in 1892, workers protested their low pay.

Factory pollution was one of the ills of the Industrial Revolution.

The Effects of Industrialization

By the turn of the twentieth century, the Industrial Revolution had transformed the United States. The country had become one of contrasts. Cities were filled with wealthy people in glamorous homes as well as desperately poor people in broken-down tenements. More than a century earlier, Thomas Jefferson had predicted the ills of industrialization. Now his grim vision could be seen everywhere. And yet, Alexander Hamilton's predictions, too, had come to pass. The United States had developed into the leading industrial nation in the world.

The U.S. Industrial Revolution ushered in a new era—one that had good aspects and bad. Between the rich and the poor grew a middle class. This group was made up of highly skilled laborers as well as people who managed factories. Some people took the knowledge they had gained while working in factories and opened stores. They sold the products they had formerly made. They also joined the middle class.

Need versus Want

The middle class produced a different kind of consumer. Members of the middle class had enough money to buy products that made life a bit easier, such as sewing machines and washing machines. These were laborsaving devices that people wanted but did not need to have.

As many of these products came on the market, middle-class families were forced to make choices. They could not afford all of them. Merchants relied on advertising to convince the middle class that the particular products they were selling were the ones to buy.

TERRIBLE TENEMENTS

But many of the factory workers who had helped America's tycoons earn their great wealth felt robbed of the American dream. These underpaid workers, many of them immigrants, lived in rundown tenements in the country's inner cities. The tenements, buildings made up of numerous housing units, served as inexpensive housing. Built close to factories or transportation, they were constructed from cheap materials. Often many families had to share a single bathroom. The builders, who were usually also the landlords, did not have their tenants' well-being in mind. They charged high rents but provided few services in return. Landlords refused to make needed repairs, to pick up garbage regularly, to keep the buildings clean, and to get rid of rats and other pests. Tenements were built next to each other and, in time, entire neighborhoods became rundown slums.

The Progressive Era began around 1890 and lasted until the United States entered World War I in 1917. During this time, reformers worked to improve social ills, including labor conditions and the lives of the poor.

Health Care

In the early twentieth century, many residents of tenements were too poor to afford any type of medical care. Because their housing was so crowded, diseases such as measles and smallpox spread quickly. However, visits to the doctor were out of the question because of the high cost. Families did the best they could to take care of their illnesses on their own. Without proper health care, however, many people—especially children—died.

Author Upton Sinclair wrote about the dismal conditions in factories in his famous work, *The Jungle*. Journalist Jacob Riis also documented the awful working and living conditions. In his book, *How the Other Half Lives*, Riis reported what he learned from those in the tenements:

> *The complaint was universal among the tenants that they were entirely uncared for, and that the only answer to their requests to have the place put in order by repairs and necessary improvements was that they must pay their rent or leave.* [1]

Some governments responded. In 1901, the New York State Tenement House Act was passed. This law forced landlords to keep up their properties, and some improvements were made. Beyond New York City, however, housing conditions in many urban areas remained dismal. Housing around many of Andrew Carnegie's steel-mill towns was described as

Tenement Exposé

Journalist Jacob Riis first wrote "How the Other Half Lives," as an 18-page article, in 1889. The piece was published in *Scribner's Magazine* and was illustrated with 18 of his own photographs. Riis was asked to expand the hard-hitting exposé on tenement life into a book, which he did in 1890. He wrote a sequel, called *Children of the Poor*, in 1892. This title delved into what life was like for the youth of neglected tenement neighborhoods. "The slum is a measure of civilization," Riis was quoted as saying. [2] In other words, as civilization progressed through industrialization, the negative aspect of slums seemed to be inevitable.

rundown at best. Filthy buildings stood surrounded by sunken sidewalks and ruined streets. Decades later, the federal government passed the Housing Act of 1949 to repair tenements and clean up slums.

SAFETY AND HEALTH REFORMS

Some reforms took years to become law. A law to govern safety standards in the workplace—the Occupational Safety and Health Act—was not passed by Congress until 1970. Pollution was another issue that was put off. Factory waste dumped into rivers polluted water, and smoke from burning coal blotted the city skies. Even so, the problem was not seriously addressed until the 1960s. Natural resources were also often carelessly wasted by big business. The environmental effects of industrialization are still a large concern today.

Women's Voices

Having worked in some of the first mills, women were key players in the Industrial Revolution from its beginning. Women were also among the most vocal reformers. They spoke out against the social ills that came out of the Industrial Revolution. Among their causes were child labor and the unfair practice of paying women less than men for equal work.

In 1900, a group of civic-minded women organized the International Ladies' Garment Workers Union. This grew to be one of the largest labor organizations to fight for labor reforms in the garment industry.

GOOD AND BAD

In his 1913 Inaugural Address, President Woodrow Wilson cited "the genius of individual men and the limitless enterprise of groups of men" that were key to the innovative period in U.S. history.[3] But he also acknowledged that some of the wonderful advancements made during the Industrial Revolution came at a great cost. Wilson said,

> With riches has come inexcusable waste. We have squandered a great part of what we might have used, and have not stopped to conserve the

The Beginning of Computers

The U.S. Industrial Revolution may have had a direct impact on the development of the computer. Every ten years, a census is taken that determines how many people live in the United States. The first census, taken in 1790, took nine months to complete. But by 1880, the population in the United States had grown so much, it took eight years to complete the census.

The U.S. Census Bureau was so concerned about how long the process had taken that it offered a prize to anyone who could streamline the system. Herman Hollerith, a native of Buffalo, New York, proposed a punch-card system for tallying the census. He invented the Hollerith desk. This card reader sensed the holes in the cards and counted them. It was an early form of computer programming.

Hollerith's system was used for the 1890 census. The process was complete by 1892, at a savings of $5 million. Following the success of his invention, Hollerith opened the Tabulating Machine Company. It eventually became International Business Machines, better known as IBM. The Hollerith desk is considered a key step in the development of computers.

*exceeding bounty of nature, without which our genius for
enterprise would have been worthless and impotent . . . . We
have been proud of our industrial achievements, but we have
not hitherto stopped thoughtfully enough to count the human
cost, the cost in lives snuffed out, of energies overtaxed and
broken, the fearful physical and spiritual cost to the men and
women and children upon whom the dead weight and burden
of it all has fallen pitilessly.*[4]

The Industrial Revolution in the United States
opened the corridors of transportation, simplified
worldwide communication, unlocked powerful new
worlds through electricity, and forever changed
workers' lives. It encouraged limitless imagination,
which gave way to technologies beyond what anyone
had thought possible. Industrialization sparked
inventions that would forever change almost every
aspect of life. It also allowed for those inventions
to be mass-produced, making them available
to everyone. As both Jefferson and Hamilton
predicted, the U.S. Industrial Revolution brought
both negative and positive effects. But all would
agree that the era forever transformed the country's
economic and social landscape.

President Woodrow Wilson recognized the positive and negative aspects of the Industrial Revolution.

TIMELINE

1787	1787	1789
Thomas Jefferson's book *Notes on the State of Virginia* is published. In it he argues to keep the United States a farm-based economy.	On August 22, John Fitch tests a steam-powered boat on the Delaware River.	Samuel Slater revolutionizes the textile industry in the United States.

1813	1825	1825
In a new kind of factory, finished cloth is produced from raw cotton under one roof.	After eight years of construction, the Erie Canal opens in New York State on October 26.	John Stevens demonstrates a steam-powered locomotive that runs on iron rails in Hoboken, New Jersey.

1790

The nation's first Patent Act is enacted on April 10.

1791

Alexander Hamilton submits his "Report on Manufactures" to Congress, which argues for industrialization in America.

1807

On August 17, Robert Fulton introduces the first commercially successful steamboat and travels up the Hudson River.

1834

The National Trades Union, the first national labor union, is founded.

1844

Samuel Morse sends a long-distance telegram for the first time on May 24.

1865

The North wins the American Civil War. The victory is due in large part to industrialization.

TIMELINE

1869	1874	1876
The transcontinental railroad is completed on May 10. People can now travel by rail across the United States.	Andrew Carnegie opens his first steel mill in Braddock, Pennsylvania.	Thomas Alva Edison opens the first industrial research laboratory in Menlo Park, New Jersey.

1892	1893	1903
Employees strike at a Carnegie steel plant in Homestead, Pennsylvania, to protest low wages and attempts to shut down their labor union.	The World's Columbian Exposition is held from May 1 to October 30.	The Wright brothers make their first successful flight on December 17 in Kitty Hawk, North Carolina.

1876

The Centennial Exhibition is held in Philadelphia to celebrate 100 years of industrial development in the United States.

1876

Alexander Graham Bell, with Thomas Watson, creates the first working telephone and makes the first phone call on March 10.

1890

The Sherman Antitrust Act, outlawing monopolies, becomes law on July 2.

1908

Ford produces his first Model T automobile on October 1.

1938

Congress passes the Fair Labor Standards Act, which sets the workweek at 40 hours and prohibits child labor.

1970

Congress passes the Occupational Safety and Health Act to regulate safety standards in the workplace.

ESSENTIAL FACTS

DATE OF EVENT

Late 1700s–1920s

PLACE OF EVENT

United States

KEY PLAYERS

❖ Samuel Slater, textiles industrialist and inventor

❖ Eli Whitney, inventor of the cotton gin

❖ Samuel Morse, creator of telegraphy

❖ Alexander Graham Bell, inventor of the telephone

❖ Thomas Edison, inventor of the practical lightbulb

❖ Andrew Carnegie, steel magnate

❖ The Wright brothers, pioneers of flight

❖ Henry Ford, creator of the mass-produced automobile

Highlights of Event

❖ Experienced textile innovator Samuel Slater came to the United States in 1789, bringing knowledge of industrial technology that helped spark the Industrial Revolution in the country.

❖ In the early nineteenth century, Eli Whitney demonstrated the value of interchangeable parts, which led the way to mass production.

❖ Francis Cabot Lowell created the shareholder corporation concept in the early nineteenth century.

❖ The completion of the transcontinental railroad in 1869 provided inexpensive transportation for people and goods within the United States. It allowed businesses to ship their merchandise and open plants throughout the country.

❖ In the late nineteenth century, Thomas Edison developed an electrical grid big enough to power major cities across the United States and introduced electricity into homes and businesses.

❖ In 1913, Henry Ford implemented the assembly-line process, which made cars affordable for the average wage earner.

Quote

"We have been proud of our industrial achievements, but we have not hitherto stopped thoughtfully enough to count the human cost, the cost in lives snuffed out, of energies overtaxed and broken, the fearful physical and spiritual cost to the men and women and children upon whom the dead weight and burden of it all has fallen pitilessly." —*Woodrow Wilson, First Inaugural Address, March 4, 1913*

ADDITIONAL RESOURCES

SELECT BIBLIOGRAPHY

Cadbury, Deborah. *Dreams of Iron and Steel*. New York: Fourth Estate, 2003.

Dudley, William, ed. *The Industrial Revolution: Opposing Viewpoints*. San Diego, CA: Greenhaven Press, 1998.

Goloby, Jennifer L., ed. *Industrial Revolution People and Perspectives*. Santa Barbara, CA: ABC-CLIO, 2008.

Hillstrom, Kevin, and Laurie Collier Hillstrom, eds. *The Industrial Revolution in America: Communications*. Santa Barbara, CA, ABC-CLIO, 2007.

Olson, James S. *Encyclopedia of the Industrial Revolution in America*. Westport, CT: Greenwood Press, 2002.

Wyatt, Lee T. *The Industrial Revolution*. Westport, CT: Greenwood Press, 2009.

FURTHER READING

McNeese, Tim. *The Robber Barons and the Sherman Antitrust Act*. New York: Chelsea House, 2009.

Pederson, Charles E. *Thomas Edison*. Edina, MN: ABDO, 2007.

Woog, Adam. *A Sweatshop During the Industrial Revolution*. San Diego, CA: Lucent Books, 2003.

WEB LINKS

To learn more about the U.S. Industrial Revolution, visit ABDO Publishing Company online at **www.abdopublishing.com**. Web sites about the U.S. Industrial Revolution are featured on our Book Links page. These links are routinely monitored and updated to provide the most current information available.

Places To Visit

Henry Ford Museum
20900 Oakwood Boulevard, Dearborn, MI 48124-4088
313-982-6001
www.thehenryford.org/museum/index.aspx
The Henry Ford Museum includes a large exhibit on the impact the
automobile has had on American life.

Slater Mill
67 Roosevelt Avenue, Pawtucket, RI 02860
401-427-8638
www.slatermill.org/museum/
Now a museum complex, the Slater Mill brings to life the early
textile industry in New England, including a replica of the original
mill wheel.

Thomas Edison National Historic Park
211 Main Street, West Orange, NJ 07052-5612
973-324-9973
www.nps.gov/edis/index.htm
Tour the private estate and laboratory of Thomas Alva Edison as
well as Edison's recording studio and photo lab, which are filled
with exhibits.

Wright Brothers National Memorial
1401 National Park Drive, Manteo, NC 27954
252-441-7430
www.nps.gov/wrbr/index.htm
The park commemorates the area where the Wright brothers
worked on developing the first airplane. Their living quarters,
laboratory, and hangar have been reconstructed on the site where
the buildings first stood.

Glossary

assembly line
An arrangement of people and equipment in which work passes to each station in a line until a product is completed.

canals
Human-made waterways connecting lakes and rivers to transport people and goods by boat.

collective bargaining
A method of negotiating working conditions, wages, and other workplace issues between an employer and employees.

horizontal monopoly
One company that has bought out all companies selling a similar product.

industrialization
The development of manufacturing on a massive scale, which greatly expands a country's economic base.

interchangeable parts
Identical parts that can be used in place of one another; interchangeable parts make mass production possible and inexpensive.

magnate
A wealthy, influential, and powerful business leader.

merger
The combining of companies or divisions within companies.

monopoly
Exclusive control of an industry, such as steel or oil, by one organization or corporation.

patent
>Rights to an invention that are guaranteed by law.

prototype
>The first working model of a proposed invention.

tenements
>Poorly maintained, poorly constructed, low-income, multifamily housing built in inner cities near industrial areas.

tycoon
>A very wealthy businessperson.

unions
>Organizations of workers, charged with the responsibility of fighting for employee rights, including better salaries, benefits, and working conditions.

vertical monopoly
>One company that has bought out every company that is needed to complete the different stages of production of its product.

SOURCE NOTES

Chapter 1. A Revolution Begins
None.

Chapter 2. Life before the Industrial Revolution
None.

Chapter 3. Textiles in America
1. Charles Dickens. *American Notes.* London, England: Chapman and Hall, 1874. 77.

Chapter 4. Transportation Improvements
1. Edwin Wilson Morse. *Causes and Effects in American History: The Story of the Origin and Development of the Nation.* New York: Charles Scribner's Sons, 1912. 112.
2. "The Erie Canal: A Brief History." New York State Canals. Canal Culture, Canal History. 16 Sept. 2009 <http://www.nyscanals.gov/cculture/history/>.

Chapter 5. Big Business
1. Theodore Roosevelt. *Theodore Roosevelt: An Autobiography.* New York: The Macmillan Company, 1913. 462–463.

Chapter 6. American Ingenuity
1. Catherine W. Zipf. *Professional Pursuits: Women and the American Arts & Crafts Movement.* Knoxville, TN: University of Tennessee Press, 2007. 53.

Chapter 7. The Communications Boom
1. Alvin F. Harlow. *Old Wires and New Waves.* New York: D. Appleton Century Company, 1936. 59.
2. Charlotte Gray. *Reluctant Genius: Alexander Graham Bell and the Passion for Invention.* New York: Arcadia Publishing, 2006. 122.
3. George P. Olsin. *The Story of Telecommunications.* Macon, GA: Mercer University Press, 1999. 221.

Chapter 8. Working Conditions
1. "Mother" Mary Harris Jones. *Women in History.* 10 Sept. 2009 <http://www.lkwdpl.org/wihohio/jone-mar.htm>.

Chapter 9. The Effects of Industrialization

1. Jacob Riis. *How the Other Half Lives.* New York: Charles Scribner's Sons, 1890. 4.

2. James F. Wikens. *Highlights of American History: Glimpses of the Past.* Chicago, IL: Rand McNally & Co., 1973. 246.

3. Woodrow Wilson. First Inaugural Address, March 4, 1913. 10 Sept. 2009 <http://www.bartleby.com/124/pres44.html>.

4. Ibid.

Index

Index Continued

ABOUT THE AUTHOR

Robert Grayson is an award-winning former daily newspaper reporter and the author of books for young adults. Throughout his journalism career, Grayson has written stories on historic events, sports figures, arts and entertainment, business, pets, and profiles that have appeared in national and regional publications. He has written books about animals in the military and animal performers as well as the environment, law enforcement, and professional sports.

PHOTO CREDITS

North Wind Picture Archives, cover, 3, 6, 13, 14, 23, 45, 52, 76, 87; Kevin Eaves/iStockphoto, 9; AP Images, 20, 35, 96 (bottom); North Wind Picture Archives/Photolibrary, 19, 24, 29, 30, 33, 39, 41, 42, 66, 70, 88, 96 (top), 97; B. L. H. Dabbs/Library of Congress, 47, 98; Library of Congress, 51, 54, 82, 95; J. Walter Thompson, 56; Hulton Archive/Getty Images, 65, 75, 99